CONTENTS

What is magnetism?

Magnetism is an invisible force found in certain types of metal or rock. Magnets can either occur naturally in the ground, or be made artificially. A magnet can pull some metals to it and show the direction of north and south.

Magnetic rock

The force of magnetism is thought to be named after a rock called magnetite. The rock is magnetic because it contains iron. Large amounts of this naturally magnetic rock were found in a place called Magnesia over two thousand years ago. Today, Magnesia is part of Turkey.

This horseshoe magnet is holding a piece of magnetite rock up in the air.

Leading the way

If a long piece of magnetite is hung on a string it points north and south. For this reason, its first use was as a compass. People called the rock lode stone, meaning leading stone, because it helped to lead people on their journeys.

The ball of this lode stone compass swivels in its stand to point to the north.

MAGNETIC METALS

Materials which are attracted by magnets are described as magnetic. Materials that are not pulled towards a magnet are described as non-magnetic.

Today, we know that four metals are magnetic. They are iron, steel, cobalt and nickel. Most magnets are made from magnetic metals such as iron and steel, but some are made from a mixture of magnetic and non-magnetic metals.

Magnets can be made into all sorts of shapes and sizes.

INVESTIGATE!

Use a magnet to test different materials such as wood, aluminium, steel, paper, wool and iron to see which are magnetic and which are non-magnetic.

All of these objects are magnetic.

THE POLES OF A MAGNET

The pole of a magnet is a place where the magnetic force is strongest. A bar magnet has a pole at each end. One of these is a north-seeking pole, and the other is a south-seeking pole.

This bar magnet has come to rest with the north-seeking pole pointing north and the south-seeking pole pointing south.

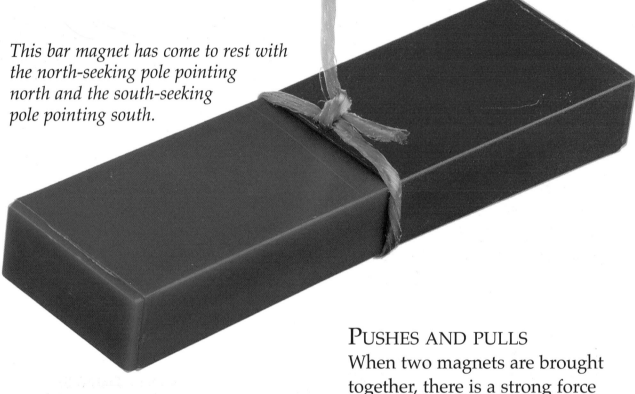

PUSHES AND PULLS

When two magnets are brought together, there is a strong force between them. The type of force depends on which poles are brought together.

Similar poles – such as a north pole and north pole – push each other away, or repel each other. When the poles are not similar – such as a north pole and a south pole, or a south pole and a north pole – they pull together, or attract each other.

North and south poles attract each other.

North and north poles repel each other.

South and south poles repel each other.

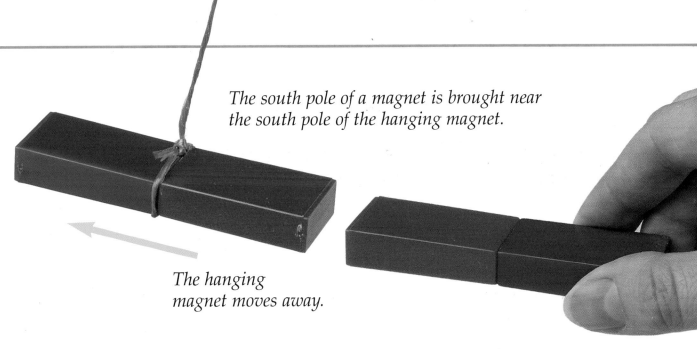

The south pole of a magnet is brought near the south pole of the hanging magnet.

The hanging magnet moves away.

MAKING A MAGNET MOVE

A hanging bar magnet will start to swing if a second bar magnet is brought close to it. If similar poles are brought together, the hanging magnet will swing away from the second magnet. If opposite poles are brought together, the hanging magnet will swing towards the second magnet.

ALWAYS TWO POLES

If you cut a magnet into pieces, each piece has a north and a south pole. It is not possible to cut a magnet in half and get two magnets with one pole each.

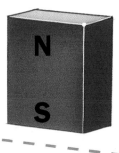

When this magnet is cut in half, each new magnet has a north and south pole.

▌INVESTIGATE!

Take two plastic toy cars and stick a bar magnet on the roof of each one. See how the cars move when you bring the poles of the magnets close together.

Magnetic force

The magnetic force of a magnet can pull magnetic materials to it if the materials are close by. The force turns the magnetic material into a magnet too.

The strength of the force

When a paper clip is brought close to a magnet, the pull of the magnetic force gets stronger. At the pole, the magnetic force is stronger than the paper clip's weight, so the paper clip is held to the magnet's end.

The magnetic force of the magnet makes the paper clip into a magnet. The paper clip can attract another paper clip to it. This second paper clip also becomes a magnet and can attract a third paper clip. The power of the magnetic force becomes weaker the further away each clip is from the magnet. When the paper clips are taken away from the magnet they lose their magnetism.

The last paper clip in the chain is such a weak magnet that it cannot make another paper clip stick to it.

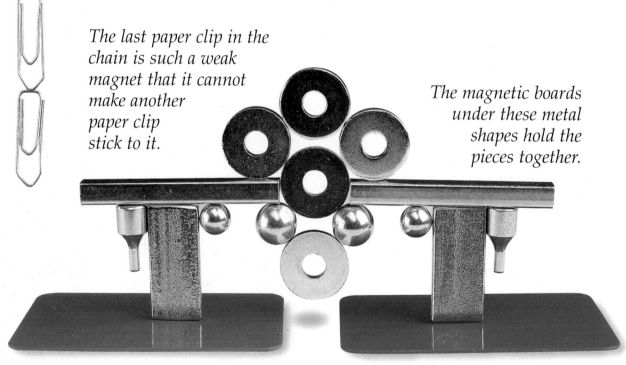

The magnetic boards under these metal shapes hold the pieces together.

PULLING THROUGH

A magnetic force can pass through non-magnetic materials and still pull on magnetic materials. If a non-magnetic material, such as a piece of card, is put between a magnet and a screw, the magnetic force still holds the screw in place. The screw can be made to move about on the card by moving the magnet on the other side.

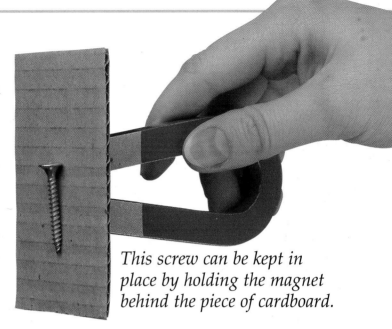

This screw can be kept in place by holding the magnet behind the piece of cardboard.

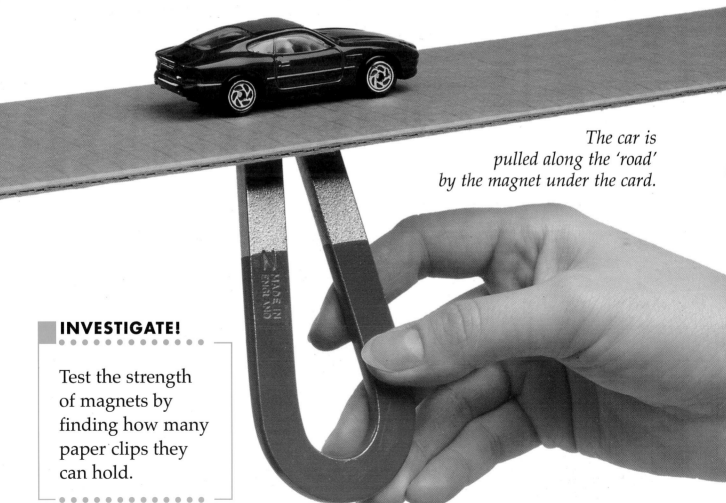

The car is pulled along the 'road' by the magnet under the card.

INVESTIGATE!

Test the strength of magnets by finding how many paper clips they can hold.

MAGNETIC FIELDS

The force which a magnet exerts on a nearby object is strongest at the magnet's poles. The other parts of a magnet, however, also exert a force. The total area around a magnet which can attract or repel magnetic materials is called its magnetic field.

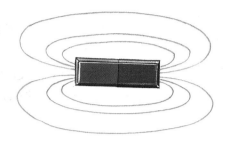

The magnetic field around a bar magnet.

MARKING OUT THE FIELD

Iron filings can be used to mark out a magnetic field. The filings are spread on a piece of paper which is then placed over a magnet. The tiny pieces of metal line up because they have been made into magnets, every one with a north and south pole. Each iron filing lines up with its north pole pointing to the magnet's south pole and its south pole pointing to the magnet's north pole.

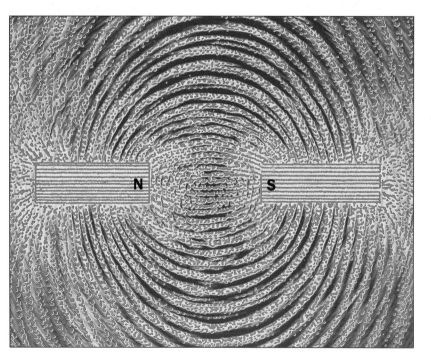

THE LINES OF FORCE

The lines the iron filings form are called the lines of force. They mark out the area, or magnetic field, on the paper where the magnetic force is strong enough to pull on the iron filings.

This image shows the lines of force between two bar magnets, their opposite poles facing each other.

THE POLES OF THE MAGNET

The lines of force are closest together where the magnetic force is strongest. Because of this, more filings cluster together at the poles than anywhere else.

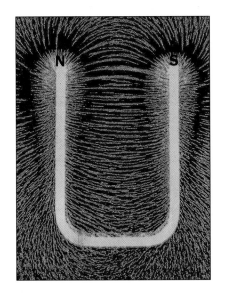

This photo shows the field around a horseshoe magnet. Where is the magnetic force strongest?

If the end of a magnet is dipped in iron filings, the filings will form spikes that stick out in all directions. The spikes show part of the lines of force that go all round the magnet.

■ INVESTIGATE!

Put a piece of paper over two magnets, placed so that their north poles face each other. Cover the paper with iron filings and see the pattern of the lines of force. Now line up the magnets so their north and south poles face each other. What happens to the lines of force?

THE EARTH'S MAGNETIC FIELD

When a magnet is allowed to swing, it lines up facing north and south. This is because it is lining up with the Earth's own magnetic field, which is called the magnetosphere. The Earth's magnetic poles lie in the north and south polar regions.

INSIDE THE EARTH

Scientists believe that at the centre of the Earth is an outer core of hot liquid iron and an inner core of solid iron. As the liquid metal moves, it makes currents of electricity which in turn make the magnetic field around the Earth.

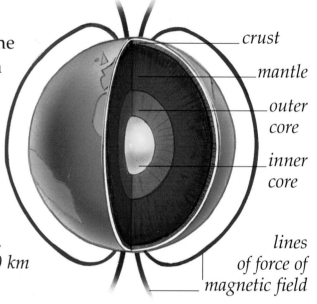

crust

mantle

outer core

inner core

lines of force of magnetic field

The movement of the iron inside the Earth causes the Earth to act like a giant magnet. The Earth's magnetic field stretches 60,000 km into space.

THE MAGNETIC POLES OF THE EARTH

At the ends of the Earth's axis are the geographic north and south poles. The north and south poles of the Earth's magnetic field, however, move in relation to the movements of the molten iron inside the Earth. A compass points directly at the magnetic poles rather than the geographic north and south poles.

This signpost shows how the Earth's magnetic south pole lies some way from the its geographical south pole.

THE COMPASS

Hikers use a compass to find their way across the countryside. The compass is made from a needle which is set on a support which lets it swing round. Beneath the needle, north, south, east and west are marked. When the needle stops swinging, it points north. Once a hiker knows which way north is, he or she can line up the map and work out which way to walk.

Compasses are used on ships. A ship's compass floats in a bowl of liquid so that it stays flat and can show accurately the direction of north and south.

This hiker is lining up his map with the north-seeking pole of his compass.

The needle of a compass is made from a magnet.

INVESTIGATE!

Set up a magnet on a piece of wood and float it in a plastic bowl filled with water. Can you find north and south?

Making a Magnet

Magnetic materials such as iron and steel are made up of millions of tiny magnetic regions, or domains. Such materials can be made into magnets when these domains are all lined up and point in the same direction.

Inside a Magnetic Material

Inside a piece of iron or steel, each of the tiny domains has a north and a south pole. When the metals are not magnetized, the domains point in many different directions.

If the metals are made into magnets, however, the domains line up with all the north poles pointing in one direction. This creates the north pole of the piece of metal. The south poles of the domains create a south pole in the metal.

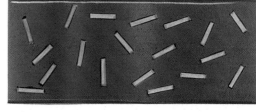

The domains in an unmagnetized piece of metal point in many different directions.

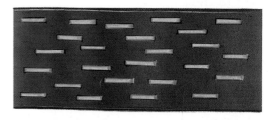

The domains in a magnetized piece of metal line up pointing north and south.

Making Weak Magnets

A nail can be made into a weak magnet by stroking it with one end of a bar magnet. The nail is stroked from one end to the other about fifty times.

Running one pole of a magnet along the side of a nail makes the domains line up, turning the nail into a magnet.

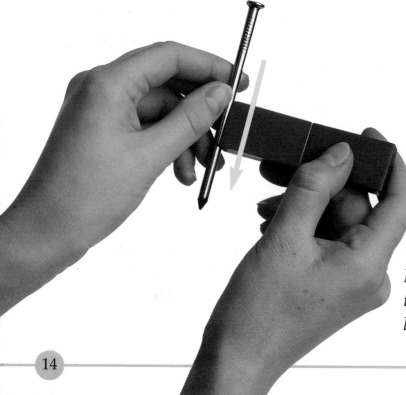

MORE WEAK MAGNETS

A pin can be made into a magnet by being placed in the magnetic field of a strong bar magnet for a few days.

A piece of iron can be made into magnet if it is lined up with the Earth's magnetic poles and left for a few days pointing north and south.

The magnetic field of the magnet makes the domains in the pin line up and turns the pin into a magnet.

Strong magnets are made from an alloy of aluminium, nickel and cobalt, known as alnico. Here, the alloy is being cast in a factory.

MAKING STRONG MAGNETS

Strong magnets have to be made in a factory. In the factory, a piece of metal is placed inside a coil of wire. A strong current of electricity is passed through the coil of wire which gives the coil a magnetic field. The domains in the piece of metal line up with the coil's magnetic field and the metal becomes a magnet.

▮ INVESTIGATE!

Make a nail into a magnet by stroking it with one end of a bar magnet.

LOSING MAGNETISM

A magnet which is looked after properly will keep its magnetism. If a magnet is heated up, or repeatedly dropped, however, it will lose its power.

WHY MAGNETISM IS LOST

A magnet loses its magnetism when its domains begin to point in different directions. As fewer and fewer domains point in the same direction, the power of the magnet falls.

Magnets should be stored with their keepers. This helps the magnets to keep their north and south poles.

The keepers at the ends of these magnets cause the domains to form a circle.

USING KEEPERS

When a bar magnet is stored, it should be placed with a magnet of similar power. The pair of bar magnets should be placed so that the north pole of one magnet is next to the south pole of the other. An iron bar, or 'keeper' should be placed across the ends of the magnets. The magnetic fields of the magnets make the domains in the keeper line up so that the keeper forms a magnet across the ends. The domains of the magnet and the domains of the keeper form a circle.

A horseshoe magnet only needs to be kept with one keeper.

KNOCKED OUT

When a magnet is dropped or hammered, the metal vibrates. These vibrations make some of the domains change their position and point in different directions. Each time a magnet is dropped, more domains move out of line and the magnet loses more power.

Banging a magnet can cause it to lose its magnetism.

HEATED UP

If a magnet is heated, the metal receives energy. Some of this energy passes to the domains and makes them move. They change positions and they move out of line. The more strongly the magnet is heated, the more magnetism it loses.

Heating up a magnet makes the domains move in many directions. This makes the magnet lose its power.

▌INVESTIGATE!

Use a magnet to make a pin magnetic. Now knock the pin with a hammer to see if you can weaken the pin's magnetism. Do not use heat.

ELECTRICITY AND MAGNETISM

When electricity passes along a wire, it makes a magnetic field around the wire. If the wire is coiled many times, the magnetic field is strengthened. Scientists and engineers make use of this fact to make magnets.

TURNING A COMPASS NEEDLE

The magnetic field around a wire carrying electricity can be shown in the following way. A wire is placed near a small compass and connected to a battery, or cell. As the electricity starts to flow through the wire, the force of the wire's magnetic field pulls on the compass needle.

The magnetic field around the wire turns the compass needle.

The force makes the needle swing so that it points across the wire. The needle moves in this way because the lines of force are arranged in rings around the wire and the needle lines up with them. When the current is switched off, the compass needle swings away again because the wire no longer has a magnetic field.

SOLENOIDS

If wire is wound into a coil, it is called a solenoid. When the solenoid is connected to a battery, electricity flows through the coils. The arrangement of the coils produces a magnetic field similar to that of a bar magnet.

A solenoid can be made by winding wire round a pencil.

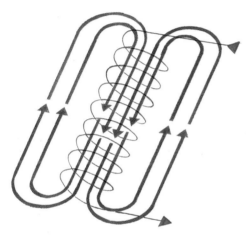

The magnetic field around a solenoid.

This steel nail has been made into a magnet by placing it in a solenoid.

If a steel nail is placed inside the solenoid and the current is switched on, the magnetic field lines up the domains in the metal and makes the nail into a magnet.

When the current is switched off and the nail is removed, the nail keeps its magnetism. It has become a permanent magnet. The more coils the solenoid has, the stronger the magnet will be.

INVESTIGATE!

Connect a wire to a battery of 4.5 volts. Place a compass near the wire and watch its needle swing.

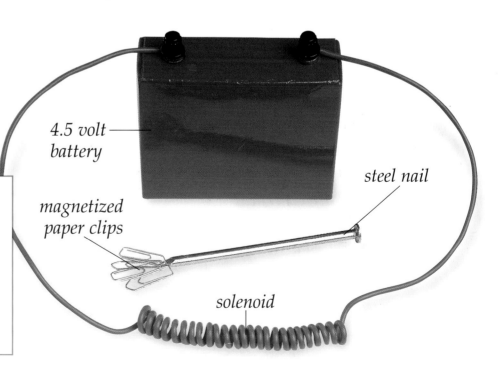

4.5 volt battery

magnetized paper clips

steel nail

solenoid

ELECTROMAGNETS

A steel bar keeps its magnetism after it has been placed in a solenoid. If an iron bar is placed in a solenoid, it loses its magnetism when the electricity is switched off. An iron bar can be used to make a magnet that can be switched on and off. This is called an electromagnet.

The domains in an iron bar when the electric current is switched on.

HOW AN ELECTROMAGNET WORKS

When the current of electricity flows through the solenoid, the domains in the iron rod line up and a magnet is made. When the electricity is turned off, the domains immediately point in many directions and magnetism is lost.

The domains in an iron bar when the electric current is switched off.

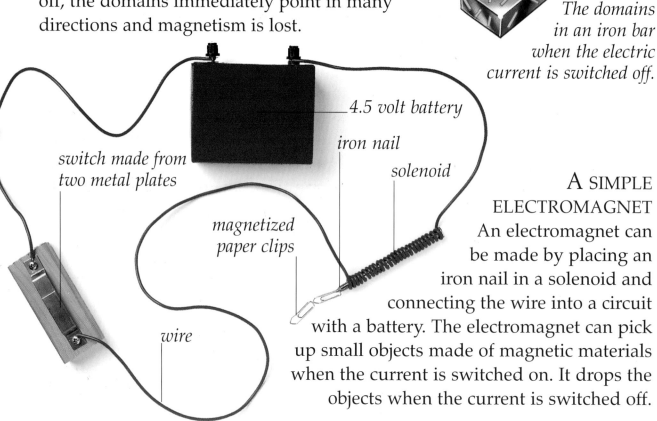

switch made from two metal plates

4.5 volt battery

iron nail

solenoid

magnetized paper clips

wire

A SIMPLE ELECTROMAGNET

An electromagnet can be made by placing an iron nail in a solenoid and connecting the wire into a circuit with a battery. The electromagnet can pick up small objects made of magnetic materials when the current is switched on. It drops the objects when the current is switched off.

The plates of the switch are touching, so electricity flows from the battery along the wire. This makes the iron nail inside the coil of wire into a temporary magnet.

A POWERFUL ELECTROMAGNET

Cars are made of steel. In a scrapyard, the old cars are stacked to save space before the metal in them is recycled. A crane with a powerful electromagnet on it is used to move the cars about. The electromagnet is made from a large coil of thick wire held in a metal case.

The powerful electromagnet on the crane can pick up a crushed car and lift it on or off the stack.

INVESTIGATE!

Set up a simple electromagnet as shown on page 20. Try coiling the wire only a few times – how strong is the magnet? Now try coiling the wire many times. Is the electromagnet now stronger?

THE ELECTRIC BELL

An electromagnet is used to make an electric bell ring. Next to the electromagnet is a piece of iron with a small hammer. There is a switch in the circuit around the electromagnet which switches the magnet on and off very quickly, making the hammer strike the bell many times.

As electricity flows through the electromagnet, its magnetic force pulls the piece of iron towards it and the hammer hits the bell.

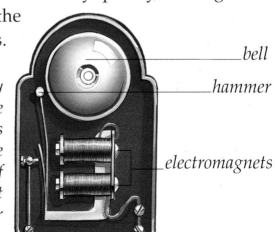

bell

hammer

electromagnets

MAKING ELECTRICITY

We have seen how electricity can be used to create magnetism. In a similar way, the magnetic field around a magnet can be used to create a current of electricity in a nearby wire.

A SIMPLE GENERATOR

A current of electricity can be made by a magnet. To show this, place a compass in or on a small box and wrap a wire around the box about 20 times to make a coil. Then make a second coil with about 50 turns which is big enough to fit a bar magnet inside it.

Pushing the magnet into the large coil of wire makes the compass needle turn. This shows that electricity has been generated.

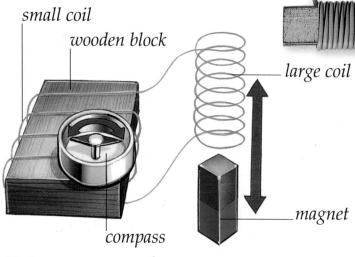

small coil
wooden block
large coil
magnet
compass

If the magnet is moved in and out of the large coil, a current of electricity flows first in one direction then in the opposite direction.

When the magnet is pushed into the coil, it generates a current of electricity in the wire. The current flows through the small coil too. The magnetic field of the current makes the compass needle turn. The magnet generates a second current of electricity when it is pulled out of the large coil.

GENERATING ELECTRICITY

The electricity we use in our homes is also generated with a coil of wire and a magnet. The magnet spins round inside the coil of wire in the generator. The magnet is connected to a shaft which has metal turbine blades. Steam, water or wind are used to push on the blades and turn the shaft to make the magnet spin.

In many power stations, fuels such as coal and oil are burnt to boil water to make steam. Other power stations are built near a reservoir of water. As the water is released from the reservoir, it flows over turbine blades on a water wheel.

An inside view of a generator, showing turbine blades and the shaft in which the magnet spins.

These turbine blades are spun by the wind. Behind each pair of blades there is an electricity generator.

INVESTIGATE!

Set up a simple generator as shown on page 22. Move the magnet to generate electricity in the wire. See how the current changes when you move the magnet slowly and then quickly.

MAGNETS AND SOUND

Sound is made by vibrating particles in the air. Microphones use magnets to change some of the energy in these vibrations into an electric current. Loudspeakers also use magnets, but to change some of the energy in an electric current into strong vibrations in the air.

A microphone may be connected to a loudspeaker or to a tape recorder.

HOW A MICROPHONE WORKS

When a sound is made, vibrating air particles form waves which pass through the grill on the microphone and push and pull on a thin metal sheet beneath it. There is a coil of wire connected to the metal sheet, and around this coil is a magnet.

coil of wire

metal sheet

magnet

Sound waves make the metal sheet and the coil attached to it vibrate. The vibrating coil moves up and down in the magnetic field of the magnet and a current of electricity is generated.

How a loudspeaker works

A loudspeaker has a coil of wire and a magnet. The coil of wire is attached to a cone-shaped piece of plastic or paper. The coil of wire receives a current of electricity which has been generated by a microphone, a tape recorder or a CD player. This current of electricity makes the coil into an electromagnet.

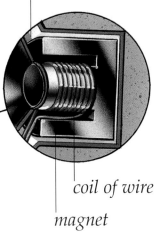

cone

coil of wire

magnet

The paper or plastic cone attached to the coil moves when there are magnetic forces between the coil and the magnet.

A loudspeaker uses a magnet to change some of the energy in an electric current into vibrations in the air so that sound is made.

The magnetic forces between the magnet and the electromagnet produce movement. The current changes very quickly and makes the coil move quickly up and down. The moving coil pushes and pulls on the loudspeaker cone and makes it move. The movement of the cone sets up vibrations in the air which move away from the loudspeaker as sound waves.

RECORDING TAPES

Tiny magnetic particles on sound and video tapes can store information about sounds and pictures. Magnetic forces are used to put the particles into patterns so that they can hold this information.

Underwater sounds are stored on the magnetic particles of the tape cassettes these divers are using.

RECORDING SOUND

The tape in a tape cassette is made of plastic covered in particles of magnetic materials. When sound is recorded, a current of electricity passes from the microphone to the recording head of the tape recorder, where there is an electromagnet.

The current passes through the coil of wire in the electromagnet producing a magnetic field as the tape passes by. The field pushes and pulls on the particles of the magnetic material on the tape. They stay in their new positions as the tape moves away from the recording head.

The electromagnet on the recording head of a tape recorder pushes the magnetic particles of the tape into patterns.

Magnets are not only useful – they also allow us a lot of pleasure.

PLAYBACK

A tape recorder has a playback head. This also has a magnetic field. When the tape is played back, it passes by the playback head. As the particles on the tape pass through the field, they make the playback head generate currents of electricity. These pass to a loudspeaker and the recorded sound is heard.

VIDEO TAPE

The particles on a video tape store information about sound and pictures. If they were arranged in one straight track, as on an audio tape, the video tape would have to move so quickly past the playback head that the tape would snap. So that the tape can be moved at a slower speed, the particles are arranged in many tracks across the tape and there are two recording and playback heads on a video machine.

Inside a video-editing studio. One of the screens shows the images, while the other shows the sound track.

■ INVESTIGATE!

Play an audio tape that is no longer wanted. Remove it and stroke it with a magnet. Now play it back again.

THE MANY USES OF MAGNETS

Magnets, electromagnets and magnetic materials can be used in many different ways – from keeping burglars away to helping trains to move. They can also be used just for fun: various toys make use of magnets, while some people decorate their fridges with fridge magnets.

MAGNETS AROUND THE HOME

The edge of the fridge door is lined with a magnet. It holds the door to the metal door frame and allows the door to be opened and closed without using a catch.

Magnets are used in burglar alarms, and electromagnets are used in 'ding dong' door bells or security door catches which work by pressing a button.

All of the objects on these two pages use magnets, from the 'hippo' fridge magnets, to the bicycle dynamo.

COMPUTER DISCS

Floppy discs are made of plastic and coated in particles of magnetic materials. When a disc is put into a computer it spins. A read/write head reads information from the disc or passes the information onto the computer's hard disc drive.

IN HOSPITAL

Many body scanners have an electromagnet which makes tiny particles inside the body make very small movements. A computer uses these movements to create a picture of the organs in the body so they can be checked for disease.

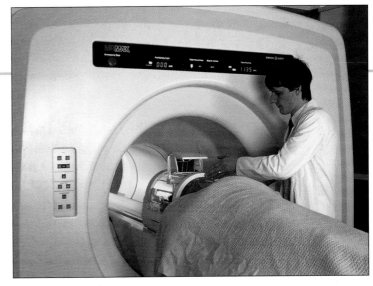

This body scanner uses an electromagnet to generate images of the patient's organs.

MAGLEV TRAIN

In Japan, electromagnets are used with some trains. The electromagnets cause the trains to float in the air and run quickly, quietly and without making polluting fumes. The train rises off its track because of the pushing power of opposite magnetic poles, then moves along because of the attraction of the steel in the track beneath it.

The Sydney monorail is an example of a Maglev train.

■ INVESTIGATE!

Loosely tape two bar magnets, one on top of the other, with the two north poles and two south poles together. Make sure you leave a small gap between them. Watch how the top magnet floats above the bottom one.

GLOSSARY

ALLOY – a mixture of two or more metals.

ALNICO – a metal alloy made from a mixture of aluminium, nickel and cobalt.

AXIS – an imaginary line which runs through the centre of the earth and which connects the north and south geographic poles.

BAR MAGNET – a magnet with a rectangular shape like a bar. It has a north pole at one end and a south pole at the other end.

BATTERY – a group of cells joined together. The battery may be made of cylindrical cells (like those used in a torch) and joined together by wires as part of an investigation, or it may be made in a factory where the cells are stacked together in a box.

CELL – a metal container which holds chemicals that can make electricity flow in a circuit.

COMPASS – an instrument which shows the position of the north and south magnetic poles. Once it has found the north pole, it can be used to find all directions.

CRANE – a machine with an arm which is used for raising and lowering objects.

DOMAIN – a tiny region in iron, steel, cobalt or nickel which acts in the same way as a bar magnet.

ELECTROMAGNET – a magnet made with a coil and a piece of iron. It only has magnetic power when a current of electricity flows through the wire.

FORCE – a push or a pull which produces movement.

GENERATOR – a device which makes electricity.

GEOGRAPHIC NORTH AND SOUTH POLES – the poles of the planet around which the Earth turns or rotates.

HIKER – a person who walks across the countryside for pleasure and recreation.

IRON – one of the four metals we know to be magnetic.

IRON FILINGS – tiny pieces of iron similar in size to ground pepper.

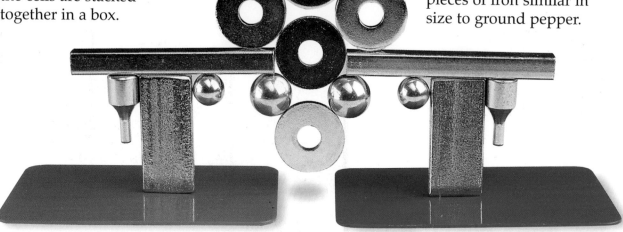

KEEPER – an iron bar which is used to preserve the magnetic power of a magnet. It is put across the opposite poles of a pair of magnets, or across the poles of a horseshoe magnet.

LINES OF FORCE – lines around a magnet which can be seen when iron filings are placed on a piece of paper which is placed over a magnet.

MAGNETIC FIELD – the area around a magnet which contains the magnet's lines of force. It is the area in which the magnetic force of the magnet can pull on magnetic materials.

MAGNETIC MATERIALS – materials which are attracted to a magnet and which can be made into a magnet.

MAGNETITE – a rock which contains large amounts of iron. It is the iron in the magnetite which makes the rock magnetic.

NON-MAGNETIC MATERIALS – materials which are not attracted to a magnet. Although they cannot be made into magnets by themselves, some, such as aluminium, can be mixed with magnetic materials and used to make magnetic alloys such as alnico.

PERMANENT MAGNET – a magnet which can keep its magnetic power for a long time.

POLE – the place on a magnet where the magnetic force is strongest.

RESERVOIR – an artificial lake in which water is stored.

SOLENOID – a coil of wire through which electricity can pass and which generates a magnetic field.

STEEL – a metal made by removing a substance called carbon from iron. It one of the four metals we know to be magnetic.

TURBINE BLADES – broad pieces of metal on which wind or water can push and turn a magnet in a generator.

VIBRATIONS – rapid movements up or down or from side to side.

WEAK MAGNET – a magnet which can only keep its power for a short time.

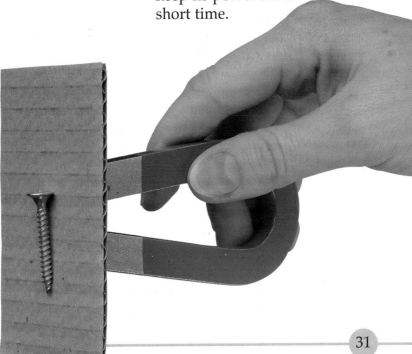

INDEX